MRG TRISHNA
and other poems

Indu K. Mallah

HAWAKAL PUBLISHERS

Published by: **Hawakal Publishers**, 185, Kali
Temple Road, Nimta, Calcutta 700049, India.

Website: www.hawakal.com
Contact: info@hawakal.com

First edition: December, 2018

Printed and bound at *S. P. Communications,*
Kolkata

Cover art: Canva
Cover Design: Bitan Chakraborty

ISBN-13: 978-93-87883-42-0

Price: INR 350/- [USD 15.00]

"If I were to choose between the power of writing a poem and the ecstasy of a poem unwritten, I would choose the ecstasy. It is better poetry."

Kahlil Gibran

CONTENTS

Deep thinking can only be attained by deep feeling.
S.T.Coleridge

*This world will pay the price not for the evil done by
the bad people,
But for the appalling silence of the good ones.*

> *Wayfarer, there is no way—*
> *Only storm-trails to the sea.*
>   *Antonio Machado*

Deep thinking can only be attained by deep feeling.
S.T. Coledridge

THE SEA AND THE HARBOUR

For a long time now,
The pendulum of my mind
Has swung between
The addiction of reading
And the discipline of writing,
From the security blanket of reading in bed,
To the challenging chill of the writing desk,
From the drug of reading novels,
To the tonic of writing them,
From the comfort-zone of reading rhymes,
To the craggy cliffs of writing poetry.

This morning,
I left the safe harbour of reading,
For the uncharted sea of writing,
With only the compass of my insight to guide me.

I found a pearl of a poem
Far from the shore.

When I returned,
The beach of my mind was strewn with sea-shells
Which echoed the rhythms of the world.

MINDSCAPE

I close the front door
And open another
To a different latitude.

Here is a country without frontiers,
Here is a landscape
Silhouetted against another sky.

The soil here pulsates with promise
And the land is peopled
Only by ideas.

I breathe deeply
Of the bracing air,
And listen to the sound of silence.

In this serene stillness
Something stirs.

A seed long deprived of nurture
By a sterile soil,
Begins to sprout.

MYSTIC MOMENT

A soul-searing book
With the eternal themes of
Human frailty, and rigid morality,
Injustice, and inter-connection.

A haunting *sangeet sammelan;*
As the maestro's voice soars into space and
beyond,
It sweeps *rasikas* to a magnetic field of
transcendental meditation.
His rendering of raag *Bhairavi*
Wings me to a sublime arc of synergy.
"Jaise dharthi megh bina,
Jaise pran Hari bina…"

At that mystic moment,
A luminous flash of insight
Meteors and ignites
A dormant volcano in my mind.

The explosion that follows

13

Reverberates through the micro
And sends shock-waves to the macro.

I am still resonating
To the after-shock
 Of that impact.

*Like the earth without clouds
Like life without Hari (God).

HIGHWAY, BYWAY

"...The first path is very easy,

Those who take this path
Lose themselves to please the world.

The second path
Is very hard.

This is the path of those who travel towards
themselves,
Who discover their own true self."

Do Raha (Cross-roads)
by Javed Akhtar

When I galloped on the highway of my life,
On my steed of invincibility,
It was always high-noon in my day;
The sun could never set on my joy,
As I rode into the challenge of the high wind,
Spurring my mount with my *joie de vivre*,
The world and its ways were always with me,
I was never alone.

Suddenly

The road dead-ended;
There was darkness at noon;
Dazed, bewildered,,
Battered, broken,
I sat by the way-side.

And then-
A friendly byway beckoned;
After a long while,
I trudged through this path,
Lost, alone.

Somewhere along this lonely road,
I found myself.

FAIRY- FLOSS AND CANDY –ROCK

She sits in her ivory-tower,
Spinning, spinning, spinning
Fairy-floss from airy froth
Into dainty daisies,
Pretty pansies,
Blood-red roses.

He heaves and chops,
Plods and ploughs,
Sowing the seeds of his visceral poetry
Into the rocky earth and the high wind.
His hands have bruised themselves
On the locked doors of her compassion.

At close of day, he brings home
A bird with a broken wing,
A hare with a spintered leg,
An orphaned baby squirrel.

Now she is a butterfly,
Delicate, diaphanous,

Now, a praying mantis,
Awaiting her prey.

Slowly his poems sprout into the whirlwind,
Etching the calligraphy of his feelings on the
sky.

One day, he slumps over his plough,
His heart full of gulped tears.
The bird with the broken wing,
The hare with the splintered leg,
Now healed with his grace,
The orphaned baby-squirrel,
Are his chief mourners.

She soon got herself another man,
And went on spinning, spinning, spinning.

FOR SHILPA

If sculpture is frozen dance,
And dance is graphic poetry,
Then music is melodious painting.

The ripples of emotion as you sang,
Danced on the sea of your face,
Echoing the waves of the ocean of your soul.

Are you sculpture,
Are you dance,
Are you music,
Or, are you a *ragamalika* painting?

Your singing exalted me
From the mundane to the sublime
On a magnetic arc ,
With you, the *vidushi*
At one end, merging with your *sadhana,*
And I, your *rasika,*
At the other, resounding to your vibrations.

Through the flow of our synergy,
We create a pulsating poem.

19

POETRY WORKSHOP

Rhyme, rhythm,
Metre, metaphor,
Alliteration, assonance,
Blank verse, free verse,
Imagery, insight...

My mind reels with impressions,
And questions:
Where does art end, and craft begin?
Can the spark of a poem be fanned by the flames
         of the furnace?
How long is the journey from the flash of insight
To the printed page?

I take a brief break-
And a deep breath;
Outside, someone is helping an old woman cross
         the road,
Someone is aiding an accident victim,
Someone else is reaching out to a challenged child.

Then the realization hits me-

The living poems are out there,
In real life,
Not between the pages of a book,
Celebrating the poetry of life.

JUGALBANDHI-1*

The mother moved silently into the *alaap,*
Cocooning it with concern,
As it seamlessly augmented the ambience;
The flute of the daughter's face
Rose in a vibrant *Bhairavi;*
The veena of the mother's visage
Played a plaintive *Bhimpalasi;*
The daughter responded with a *Darbari*
           through her eloquent eyes.
The mother pleaded with a poignant *Malkauns*
On the strings of her emotions.
The daughter replied with a *Pahadi,*
At once playful and pensive,
Through the *sruthi* of her stance;
Her mother concluded the recital with *raag*
           Yaman,
Majestic, dedicated, devoted.

In the background, the father fostered
A harmonic resonance-field
With the tanpura of his protection.

JUGALBANDHI-2
For Lachhu

The *vasantham* of your smiling face
Thawed the shishir of my frozen heart;
The verdant veena of your body
Played a joyous *sudha saveri*;
The sitar of my heavy heart
Responded with a mournful *malkauns.*

Your veena then broke out
In a vivacious *janaranjini;*
 My tired sitar replied
With a poignant *bhimpalasi.*

The diamonds of your eloquent eyes
Outshone those in your ears,
As they danced a scintillating *mohanam*
To the plaintive poetry of my *marwa.*

Long-lost sister of my soul,
The throbbing instruments of our beings
Orchestrated a *jugalbandhi,*

Now slow, now sprightly,
Now wistful, now hopeful,
Now mundane, now sublime,
In a celebration of our kindred spirits.

*Jugalbandhi-a duet, either vocal, or instrumental.
(Terms in italics are names of different ragas in
Hindustani classical music)

A TALE OF TWO TRAVELLERS

One talks about flights and time-zones,
The other thinks about flights of fancy
Which are not time or space-bound,
For he travels in his mind.

One speaks of *caviar* and *foie gras,*
The other rolls tropes on his tongue.

One holds forth on *single malt* and *Bas Armagnac*
Chenin blanc and *Pinot Noir,*
The other gets high on metre and metaphors.

One mentions mind-boggling scenery,
The other visualizes soul-stirring imagery.

One compares the fares of different flights,
The other reflects that his are always free.

One is earth-bound, though she is flying,
The other soars above the cloud-line,
Though he is on the ground.

Two travellers trapped
In the time-capsule of marriage.

FIRE

"Some day, after we have mastered the winds,
the waves, the tides and gravity...we shall
harness the energies of love. Then for the
second time in the history of the world, man
will have discovered fire."

Tielhard de Chardin.

I have known the spark of first fire,
I have known the burning heat of a
blazing fire,
I have seen the mellow glow of embers,
I have seen the flickering flames of a
fading fire.

My eyes have been stung by the smoke
from a dying fire;
I have tried to warm my icy hands
In the afterglow of ashes.

Now I light the lamp in the light-house
of my tempered love,
So that lost travellers
May find their way home
By the rays of its flame.

26

SHIPS THAT PASS IN THE NIGHT

A brief encounter,
A chance meeting,
A frisson of friendship,
A fleeting glance,
A mute nuance,
A quivering vibration,
The silent hand-clasp-
None of them last,
But they change my chemistry forever.

POETRY FOR BREAKFAST

I came down to breakfast
The day of the poetry-festival;
It was a buffet-breakfast as usual.

I went from the juices to the fruit,
From muesli to toast,
From eggs-boiled, fried, scrambled,
To sausages,bacon and ham,
Iddlies and dosas,
Coffee and tea.

The waiters waited patiently.
"Looking for something ma'am?" one
ventured;
"Can I help you?" Another offered.
Perhaps even I didn't know what I was
looking for.
Then suddenly it caught my eye.
I made a bee-line to the chafing-dish
marked "Poetry."
Its vibrations struck a chord within me,

And I heard the heart-beat of an unborn poem
Even before I opened it.

"Shall I boil it, toast it or fry it ma'am?"
Asked the waiter behind the counter.
He didn't know what hit him when I replied:
"You don't have to do a thing-its already germinating in my soul,"
Dancing out of the dining-room,
Pen and pad at the ready.

Soon the poem sprouted
And my words winged windwards.

WILD-FLOWER

This flower will not bloom when it is told,
It will not be confined to its bed,
It will smile at its neighbor,
Borrow the sugar of sunshine
From another,
Lean over the wall to see where
The scent is coming from,
Send a tendril to the tree next door
For a sleep-over.

It will not trip to a rhyming or metered tread,
Nor wear the strait-jacket of rigid
regimentation,
Or formal figures of speech;
It has its own wardrobe of
Images, textures, cadences,
And a perfumery of nuances.

It is a free spirit,
Which needs its own space,
Its own pace,
And its own piece of sky.

SHOOTING –STARS

The applause nearly shattered the small-
screen;
A wave of nostalgia swept over him
As a clip of himself receiving a trophy at
an earlier World Cup series
Was flashed across the screen;
A fleeting fragment of memory...
He switched on the light, and poured
himself another drink.

She entered the auditorium unrecognized,
She sat in the shadows, ignored;
She watched the dancer on the sage,
Remembering an earlier time,
A kinder clime...

He stood up for the standing ovation
For the author on the dias at the litfest;
He had an intense sense of *déjà vu*
As he wandered to the book-stall;

For the millionth time he wondered why
he had come,
Especially when the attendant handed
over
The unsold, shop-soiled copies of his
book to him.

The same season, the same 'sky',
Only the 'stars' were different;
Who would believe that she had once
been the brightest in the
constellation?
The luminous lights on the stage
Did nothing to dispel her desolation
As she fought the mosquitoes of
memories.

Outside, a shooting-star arced across the
void.

PRISM

The lamp of your being shattered
When the flame that lit it
Was quenched too soon.
What irony made you name her Jyothi?

You lived in darkness,
Closing your eyes, your mind
To the gentle light of the stars,
Crying for the brightness of the sun.

But look, there is light behind you,
Light before you,
Light all around you-
You are surrounded by a sea of light.

The flame of your lamp burns
In a dozen different dimensions now-
One ray is refracted
Into a challenged child from a chawl,
Riding a horse in a high-school,

Another, into a boy from a basti
Receiving an award on Independence
Day;
A third into a girl from a slum,
Who is winging her way to the sky.

And *you,* dear activist, are the prism.

ACCOLADE

Each time I face an audience,
I do not expect an accolade.
One ripple,
One reverberation,
One *frisson* of fellowship
Are all I need.

If I touch a chord in one person's heart,
Strike a note in another's mind,
Pluck a string in someone's psyche,
It is enough for
The instrument of my being
To start pulsating.

One kindred spirit reflecting my views,
One stranger tuning to my wave-length,
The sound of just one hand clapping,
Set my net of wings aflutter.

My sensitive son,
You distilled the essence of my feelings
When you said:
"That's what its all about."

ASYLUM

"Ring the bells that still can ring,
There's no perfect offering;
There's a crack in everything,
That is how the light gets in."

Leonard Cohen.

The man with the splintered psyche,
The woman with the raped reality,
The child with the volcanic history,
The family with the earth-quaked
geography.

The mother with enduring empathy,
The husband with infinite understanding,
The care-giver who is the well-spring of
kindness,
The maestro in the art of healing.

The light filters through the filigree of
feelings and perceptions,
The troubled waters of humanity flow
below,
The canopy of compassion covers all.

THE MAKING OF A POEM

"I see the delegates from the poetry-fest
frequenting your shop–
Do you sell the ingredients for poetry
here?"
A pause.
"Okay- I want a kilo of creative clay,
A quarter- kilo of imagery,
A quarter- kilo of metaphors,
A hundred gms. of alliteration,
And a hundred gms. of assonance."

" Imported or Indian?"
"What's the difference in price?"
"Depends on the make-
American will be double the Indian price,
British will be quadruple."
"What about continental?"
"We don't have stocks just now,

But we're expecting a fresh stock next
week."
"Give me the best-
Give me British,
For I want to make a poem in the
Queen's English."

A week later-
"You've cheated me-
The ingredients you gave me are fake-
I'm going to report you for fraud."

"Be my guest mister,
"But you forgot the spark that lights a
poem."
"Why didn't you give it to me?
A shake of the head-
"You can't buy it over the counter,
Go to that hospital down the road,
Spend more time in the children's ward,
And the psychiatric ward;
You will get enough sparks
For a whole collection of poems."

THREE FAMILIES

The first family live in a laughter-lit home
With a foundation of hospitality,
A roof raftered with a dream,
And a lintel festooned with love.

They share food
Cooked with caring,
Served with warmth,
And garnished with a smile.
Meal-times are fun-times,
Convivial, cordial;
They eat together,
Pray together,
Stay together.

The second family reside in a multi-
storyed mansion
Built with hollow bricks of aloofness;
The members have their own space,
Do their own thing-
With smart-phones and i-phones,

Lap-tops, and i-pads,
Hi- fis and wi- fis
Which have taken over their lives.

They have micro-waved meals
When it suits them,
Eyes glued to the small-screen or i-pad,
Ears glued to i-phones.
The main medium of communication
Is through messages on the door of the
fridge.

The writing on the wall of aloneness is
clear:
They are destined to different planets
Of the heart,
The mind,
The spirit.

The third is a gurukula family;
It is not linked by blood,
But by bonds of brother-hood and sister-
hood,
Vibrations and vision;
The members are leaves of the spreading
tree of the guru's grace,
Nurtured by the roots of life's enduring
values,
Protected by the branch of a Bhayya's
arm,

Evolving together towards a different
dawn.

At dhyanam-time, Gurus's voice intones:
"Mata Parvati Devi,
Pitha Devomaheshwara,
Baandhava Shiva bhakthashcha,
Svadesho bhuvana trayam."

My mother is Parvati,
My father, Devo Maheshvara
The devotees of Shiva are my kinspeople,
The three worlds are my home.

THE GAZELLE

A tremor of tension is enough
To etch the calligraphy of hurt
On your eloquent eyes;
A raised voice,
For a fugitive frisson of fear
To make your tender body tremble.

Just a hostile look between your parents
Makes a tremulous tear
Linger on your lustrous lashes;
The sound of a promise breaking
Sends your fragile world crashing.

Pawn of two beings,
Who, having once lived in a world of
           their own,
Now dwell in parallel planets,
What right did they have to give you life,
Only to make of you a sounding-board
           for their clashes?

If you were a buck,
You could be called a whipping-boy,
But you are a delicate doe,
And a baby one at that.

How long before you seek refuge
Elsewhere?

THE OTHER BANK

I stand by the roiling river,
A fairy blue-bird beckons across the water,
But I have to wade through the mud and the mire
To reach the other bank.

I have to
Swim through the sea of sorrow
To reach the other shore;
Cut through endless red tape
To reach the other side;
Dig deep into the earth
With my bare hands ,
To reach the spring of insight;
Fight mental, emotional violence
To reach the core of myself;
Shut out the din and the dissonance
To hear the inner music.

I have to plod through long spells of the mundane
To reach the sublime.

Will it always be like this?
Is there no easy path?

WHEEL-CHAIR

This has been her caravan for years,
This has been her home and her world for longer
than she can remember,
This is her throne,
And she is the queen of all she surveys.

It was not always like this-
She smiles bitterly at the memory
Of herself somersaulting through life,
The memory of her encounter with the wheel-
chair-
How she had loathed it, and rebelled against it...

Now, like the Prisoner Of Chillon,
She is loth to leave her cell;
Her smart-phone, her i-pad, and her tablet are at
hand,
As is her TV remote.

Now, she sits by the window, leafing through
memories;

The fading light slowly turns her pages of
thoughts.

The microcosm zooms into the macrocosm
At the flick of a switch.

LANGUAGE

How many languages do you know?
"I know two Indian languages, and two
foreign."
"I can speak three, and read in two."
"I can speak six, and write in one."

I do not answer.
What about the lingua franca of silence?
Of actions?
Of feelings?

And what about the language of pictures?
The graphic imagery which is universal,
Which even the illiterate can read?

And I have said nothing
About the shoreless seas of insight.

TRAVELLING LIGHT

I was late reaching the air-port
For no fault of mine,
But I felt heavy
Bearing the burden of another's fault.

At the check-in counter I was told that my
baggage was over-weight.
I had the option of paying for the extra
freight,
Or unloading the extra weight.
"I'll jettison my tension, " I said.
But that was not enough.
"I'll off-load my grievances, resentments and
bitterness, " I added.

"Your baggage still exceeds the weight
allowed."
The officer was implacable.
I then decided to discard my burden of guilt
for others' hang-ups.
At last my bags were checked in.

But I had to cross the last barrier.
My cabin-bag had to be cleared.
"There is Explosive Material here , Madam,"
I was told in Capital Letters.
"There is pent-up anger,
Festering resentment,
Cankerous grudges."
"Alright, unload it all," I said.

By the time my bag was cleared, the plane
took off.
"You've missed your flight, Madam," said the
attendant.
"No, I haven't," I countered,
And floated, as free as a feather,
As weightless as a wish,
Buoyed up by the incredible lightness of my
being
Towards the departing plane.

As I boarded it by the skin of my teeth,
I felt like the boy in the folk-tale
Who was paid with a lump of gold for seven
years of labour,
And who traded it in turn, for a horse, a cow,
a pig, a mill-stone,
Which he threw into the well
And ran home to his mother,
Light in body, mind, and spirit.

CLOSURE

I searched for closure from hurt,
I found another direction;
I looked for closure from injustice,
I glimpsed a new beginning.

I quested closure from grief,
I was linked to an inter-connection;
I sought closure from despair,
 I happened upon a hope-tinted dimension.

I am still looking for closure.

LITFEAST

A friend dropped by the other day;
We chatted awhile,
Then I noticed it was lunch-time;
"Sorry, my cupboard is bare," I said,
"I haven't been to the market this week."
"I've had a late breakfast, " she said.

"It's the litfest season,", I replied,
"I can offer you a *litfeast.*"

For starters I served some haikus,
Followed by short-story soup,
The first course was a play,
With dialogue for two.
The main course was a powerful novel,
From which we read excerpts.

Dessert was a layered poem,
With textures of allusion,
Sandwiched with the cream of imagery,
Garnished with nuts of metaphors,

Slivers of similes, and a cherry of a punch-line.
I served it with a rich sub-text sauce.

BIO-DATA

These are only facts,
These are only bones,
There is no flesh, no blood,
There are no feelings.

This is only a negative in black-and-white,
There is no colour here;
This is cold and lifeless,
There is no warmth, no heart.

This is only a sheet of paper,
If torn to shreds, I would break to pieces,
If thrown into the fire, I would burn
If I was there.

Soul-mate, you said:
" I could not see you."
How could you,
When I am not there?

FOR BABITA

In the no-man's land between night and day,
A soul breaks free of its clay;
In the pre-dawn hush of a winter's chill,
Is heard a lament of loss.

How ,when, WHY,
Was a tender sapling felled
Before it became a tree?

Anguished cries rend the air;
The scorching smell of suffering smoulders;
A bewildered girl bows her head to destiny.

Tears, blood,
Time, space…
Somewhere along the desolate way
A flower becomes fruit;
In the gold-tinted dawn of a summer's day
Is heard a new-born's cry,
Writing across the tablet of time
A heartening haiku of hope.

"This world will pay the price not for the evil done by the bad people,
But for the silence of the good ones."

SILENCED
(For Gauri Lankesh)

They sought to censor me,
But my words flew forth as seeds,
Sprouting as print on page.

They tried to smother me,
But my breath burst out
In a telling statement.

They strove to silence me,
But my voice gushed out in a jubilant song;
They aimed to stop my heart-beats,
But my heart broke loose on the wind.

They thought they'd killed me,
But my ideas are blowing in the whirlwind.

TWO NATIONS , TWO LEADERS

One was a visionary
Who spent twenty-seven years in prison,
Carving the image of freedom for his nation
On the soft-ware of his psyche.

The other was a fighter
Who freed his country from its oppressors
But choked its breath
For thirty-seven despotic years.

The first was an elected leader,
Who sculpted the clay of his country
Into a model of democracy;
He stepped down gallantly when his term was
over,
Paving the way for his successor.
When he died, the world wept.

The other clung to the reins of power
And drove his people to desperation;

He personified the tyranny of the once-
oppressed.
When he was forced to resign,
The country celebrated a second deliverance.

Both are the sons of the continent
Whose credo is: " *I* am, because *we* are."

NIGHTMARE

Last night I had a dream-
The right arm of our country was amputated
at the shoulder,
Her left arm was dislocated;
There were bullet-holes of hatred
Throughout her body-politic,
Cancerous cells of communalism
Were seeping into the veins of her rivers,
And a demon from the left,
And a dragon from the right
Were pointing guns to her head.

I woke up with pounding heart,
To find it was no dream—
My worst night-mare had come true.

MAPS

I do not like maps-
They are too flat:
Give me the undulation of mountains,
The waves of the ocean,
The silhouettes of the trees.

I do not like maps-
They have no sound,
Give me the music of the rivers,
The whisper of the wind,
The rhythm of the rain.

I do not like maps-
They are cold and unfeeling,
Give me the benison of the sun,
The caress of the breeze,
The softness of petals,
The brush of wings.

I do not like maps-
They have no people;

Give me the laughter of children,
The vibrations of fellow-ship,
The unspoken bond beyond boundaries.

Above all, I do not like maps,
Because I do not like borders.

WHERE IS HUMANITY HIDING?

When I was a child,
Humanity was a river-
We splashed our faces,
We sprayed each other with its sweet waters.

It lived in the kind face of a stranger,
In the form of a class-mate called Zakia,
In the face of a school-mate called Heather,
In the smile of a soul-mate called Shireen.

It was an under-ground shelter,
A net-work of roots,
Of relationships.

Somewhere it got lost-
Was it in the desertification of values,
In the avarice for money, for power,
In the evil of ego?
In the suspicion leading to
The hydra-headed hatred of the Other?

Where does humanity hide
When a woman is gang-raped,
A man is lynched,
When a bomb is blasted?
Does she hide her face
Behind a purdah of shame?
Has she gone to her father's house on the
moon,
Sickened by the violence on earth?
Or-
Dreaded thought-
Is Humanity dead?

Perhaps, just perhaps,
She is still alive,
Hiding somewhere,
Waiting.

RAMANAVAMI

Today is Ramanavami:
The air is painted in festive hues,
The earth resounds with temple bells and
       peoples' prayers
And the sky showers blessings of rain-drops
From the sprinklers of clouds.
People offer puja in peaceful groups,
And the pujari blesses them: "May all be well,
May the canopy of peace protect all."
All is well.

Today is Ramanavami:
Gaudy streamers. Garish lights.
Raucous music ripping the rituals:
Shouting hawkers. Jostling crowds.
Pushing devotees breaking queues.
Blazing sun. Dizzying noise.
Drunken brawls. Building tension.
Rama, the prasad in my palm turns to poison
      on my palate.

Today is Ramanavami.
The air is rife with rifle shots,
The skies are clouded with intolerance
The smell of violence smoulders in the air.
Hurtling bombs, burning trains.
Murderous mobs. Innocent victims.
Partisan politics. Apathetic attitudes.
Corroding corruption. The ethos of
        exploitation.

O Rama where is your Ramrajya?

TWO FUNERALS

The one touched lives, and alchemized them,
The other poisoned lives, and blighted them;
The one ignited minds with wings of fire,
The other ignited bombs with hatred and
venom.

One soared above the cloud-line, borne by his
ideals,
The other grovelled on the ground, bound by
his bigotry;
The one was the People's President, missile-
man, and mentor,
The other was a depraved, hard-core terrorist.

One entered a higher consciousness
Doing what he loved best to do,
It is a silent testimonial that his birth-place,
his resting-place,
Is a place of pilgrimage;
The other was justly confined to the gallows.

Two funerals-but a cosmos apart;
One of a visionary leader, revered and loved,
The other of a sub-human convict, cursed
and hated.
The only common denominator was their
gender and 'religion.'

WORLD WOMEN'S DAY

I switch on the TV,
And see awards being given to women of worth;
I open the paper,
And head-lines about 'Women's Day' greet me.

Parliament pays lip-service to women's reservation
Tokenism is accorded to women-pilots
And women terror-fighters.
All day long, cosmetic gestures are made to mark
the day-
Sweets and gifts are distributed,
Mikes are held in front of women.

Later-
I switch on the TV,
And a news-clip of a girl being raped and burned
sears me;
I open the paper,
And a head-line hits me-
"Sudanese soldiers allowed to rape women in lieu
of wages."

The message, the spirit of World Women's
Day
Is junked with old newspapers, what's app
messages, and scraps of food;
And women's voices are stifled-

Until next year.

Plus ça change, plus c'est la même chose.

FREEDOM 70?

Today is our 70th. Independence Day-
Speeches are made,
Our National flag is hoisted,
Awards are given,
Sweets distributed,
There is celebration everywhere.

 Reports relay events across the country-
The Prime Minister's speech from the Red
　　　　Fort,
The pomp and pageantry of diverse
　　　　cultures…
And in the back-ground, the collage of
Pandit Nehru giving his Tryst With Destiny
　　　　speech.

Later, in 'Breaking News',
Images of violence in the Valley,
Build-up of tanks along our borders,
A man being lynched for an imaginary crime.
What irony informs our commemoration?

Where is the celebration for the martyrs'
          families?

 My mind goes back to that first
          Independence Day,
When the air was tinged with patriotism, and
          idealism;
What a kaleidoscopic riot of colour, sound,
          emotion
Jostling in an ecstasy of elation!
What a euphoric experience!

Alas! Bapuji, today, men are morphing into
          monsters,
And people have become pawns of a
          poisoned politics;
Panditji, your beloved Kashmir has become a
          killing-field;
Gurudeb our country is increasingly
Being broken by narrower domestic walls,

I am not used to the vocabulary of violence,
The grammar of guns;
Give me the magic ambience of that first
          Independence Day.

BORDERS

Today is World Poetry Day,
But reports proclaim the killing of a
Palestinian poet;
Today is World Music Day,
But head-lines announce the shooting of a
Sufi singer.

Today is World Human Rights Day,
But the small-screen is splashed with blood-
shed, cracked with gun-shots;
The river of blood flows through the whole
body,
How should a limb survive if its blood-supply
is blocked?

Borders do not exist on the earth;
They exist only on maps;
Borders do not exist in poetry or music,
They rear their ugly heads only in people's
perceptions.

The sun shines on the whole world,
The breeze knows no barriers,
Barbed-wire fences cannot divide rain,
They divide only people's minds.

TANGENTIAL
(For David Whyte)

I thought I had turned sideways into the light,
And disappeared into a different domain
But…I found myself trapped
Between the crags of jealousy and injustice.
Might still rules over right.
"It's the way of the world Mom, says my son."

Seers, whence came your vision?
One, close to home, turned to the light of
non-violence,
Another, in the Dark Continent followed him,
And yet another, in the New World
Did likewise, before his flame was quenched.

In the Land of the Shamrock,
A mythic race of mystics,
Besieged by barbarians,
And forced to fight,
Won once, twice, but the third time,
Insighting the impending,

Turned sideways into the fading light,
And disappeared through a rent in the rocks,
Or so the legend says.

Down Under, lived the Pacifist of Parihaka,
Who was a prophet of peace.
He it was, who taught his people
To turn to the power of passive resistance.

For the great ones, this shift of stance
Could not have been easy;
But they knew it was the only way by which
Dharma could prevail.

I thought I had turned tangentially to the
time,
And disappeared into a different dimension,
But... I have a long way to go.

Wise ones, where in the Cosmic Design
Are you pulsating?
Show me your vision,
Send me your resonance,
Infuse me with your strength.

THE PARTY

At first glance,
It was a party like any other,
But a second look revealed
That it was a party like no other;
It was a pent-house party, a *theme* party,
And the theme was very topical;
The name of the game was exploitation.

The decorations were stylized skulls and
bones
Strung out on stretched-out, flayed feelings.
The lights were yanked from human eyes;
A banner of skin proclaimed: "Might over
Right"
And the stench of corruption filled the air.
The hostess wore a gown of greed,
Liberally sprayed with "Avarice."
The host was chewing a wad of currency
notes
And bonsaied bearers served canapés of
crushed hopes.

The guests were a cross-section of society:
The religious fundamentalists made a bee-line
For the dish of dogma;
The opportunists to the dish of expediency,
The terrorist to that of explosives,
While the politician headed to the dish
labelled
"Opportunism."
I noticed all the dishes were garnished
generously
With shredded currency-notes.

In the periphery hovered a group of
translucent shadows;
They were the creative artists
Sipping glasses of rust-coloured liquid;
"Where's your glass?" they asked me
As I walked up to them.
You must bring your own cocktail of blood
and tears
Laced liberally with despair
If you want to join us."

A little distance away,
Some poets were making a bon-fire of their
ideals;
I rushed to stop them, but it was too late.
Close by, some people were raping the Earth-
Mother;

A group of women dressed in sack-cloth and
ashes
Were beating their breasts and singing a dirge
for the death of hope;
Elsewhere someone was auctioning someone
else's soul.

Nauseated by this sick scenario,
I rushed to the rest-room and threw up;
The bile was bitter in my mouth
And the basin was red.

Turning to return,
I pressed the elevator button,
And found myself
Trapped between the floors of night-maring
and waking.

NON-POLITICAL CONFERENCE

The faces were familiar,
Except for a few;
The ambience was familiar-
Silks and selfies,
One upwomanship,
Hierarchy and ego-trips,
The stench of sycophancy.

The agenda was familiar too,
And so was the hidden one;
Only the venue was new.

Was it the haze of the heat,
Or my imagination
Which projected an image of the chair-person
As Nero fiddling while Rome was burning?

The most important issues, including human
rights,
Were swept under the bulging carpet,
On the pretext of the NGO being a-political.

But what about the politics of power which
pervaded everywhere,
Permeating even the patterns
Of the curtains and upholstery?

The personal is political.

NEW AGE VIOLENCE

"Age of terrorism",
"Age of violence",
"Age of intolerance".
Violence spews out of space and cyber-space,
It contaminates our water, our food,
It poisons the very air we breathe.

But what of mental terrorism?
Emotional volence?
The war of words?
The battle of one-upmanship?
The sword-clash of egos?
The poison of power-politics?

This language of hostility, scripted by Might,
Is not New Age,
Only, it is now taking on virulent new forms.

FROM FETTERS SET FREE

"If I had to carry the burden of hatred and
bitterness outside these gates, I would
continue to be in prison."

                         Nelson Mandela.

I have been in prison for seven years,
Seven bleak, bitter years;
Seven, the magical, black-magical number of
myth and fairy-tale.
A prison bricked with bitterness,
Barbed-wired with resentment,
Poisoned by the politics of injustice.

I have been shackled
To rankling rancour
Which has eaten into my flesh
And corroded my mind.

Now, by coincidence or connectivity,
A new path beckons,
Leading to a parallel plane.

Now I am from fetters set free,
Now I am an unchained wish
Upon the wings of the wind.

OF WORK-OUTS AND BURN-OUTS

Six o'clock:
Time to turn and dream
Of kitty-parties culminating
In yet another club-night.

Sic o'clock:
The sirened start to a stressed-out day,
Guilt over lost time in exhausted sleep;
The day dawns demandingly.

Eleven o'clock:
Time for tea,
Plum-cake and petty-politics,
Samosas and scandals.

Eleven o'clock.
Time for the water-lorry;
Queues and quarrels,
Hunger and harassment.

Three o'clock:
Aerobics class. Salsa music.
Work-outs and weight-lifts,
Comparing notes on maids and chauffeurs.

Three o'clock.
Washing clothes, swabbing floors.
Lifting loads of grass and fire-wood
And weights of worries and pressing
        problems.

Five o'clock:
Walking the dog on three-inch heels,
Counting calories burnt per hour,
Hurrying home to dress for dinner.

Five o'clock:
Pulling the calf on cracking soles,
Milking the cow and trudging home,
Cooking, cleaning, washing.

Six o'clock:
Crunching canapés, gorging gossip,
Cigarette smoke in the cocktail circuit.
The burnt-out ends of smoky days.

Six o'clock:
Smouldering wood and hungering pangs,
Acrid smoke of burnt-out hopes,
The smell of dank in the dingy room.

Eleven o'clock:
The night is young:
Another drink. Another dance.
And another game of one-upwomanship.

Eleven o'clock:
A coughing child, a drunken husband;
A breaking back, a broken spirit,
Ignorance of terms like work-outs and burn-
        outs.

HOMAM

Om agne…
Tvayi visaye iti samidho juhomi
Aham ityajam juhomi…
(I sacrifice unto you my sense-cravings;
I also sacrifice my ego.)

Your parents are performing a homam
In the homa kundam of your home,
Made with the bricks of the walls
They have built between them,
Crushing you in the middle.

They light the fire with the sticks of your
feelings,
They chant mantras of the rhythms of your
pain,
They offer grains of desires to Agni–
Are they theirs, or yours?

The ego they sacrifice

Through the oblations of your tears,
Are they theirs, or yours?

As they offer the wood of the body to the
fire,
You feel *your* body burning,
For you are the *bali*.

Pawn of two people,
Who, having once loved,
Now seek revenge on each other,
Whom will you choose,
Your father or your mother?
Or will you choose a third option?

Will you grow a skin over your wound
Which will never heal,
But only fester and throb,
With bristles on both sides,
Which will smart within, and without?

Will you hide your hurt in hell-holes,
Will you seek solace in drink and drugs,
Will you turn your rage against the world,
And hurl the bomb of your fury against
Society?

Perhaps, when you are 'mending' in a remand
home,
Your parents will perform a *yajna*.

SILENT SCREAM

Baby Doll,
A doll for you,
Just like you,
On your birthday.

Barbie doll,
You're a big girl now,
A 'gift' for you,
From an 'uncle.'

Guilty girl,
You're forced to wear
A skin of guilt
For another's crime.

You can scream,
But it will only be
A silent scream
For you can never voice your pain.

PARTY GAMES

Exotic food, heady drinks,
'Non-veg' jokes,
Bomb-blast of laughter:
The scenario is familiar.

A snide remark,
A sarcastic sneer,
An aggressive stance:
The scene shifts.

Rapier-thrust wit,
Sabre-sharp repartee,
He draws first blood,
She responds with a whip-lash of wounding words.

The rules are implicit:
Hit below the belt,
Cut off your opponent in mid-sentence,
One up(wo)manship -that's the name of the game.

Breathe in the hot air

Polluted by power-politics;
Help yourself to hostility
Miscalled hospitality.

There are no winners:
Here is no blood-shed
In this battle of egos.

But this too is violence.

THE FRONTIER OF THE MIND

At the frontier of the mind,
Where my views end, and yours begin,
Craggy cliffs of prejudice parade.

At the frontier of the mind,
Where your gender ends, and mine begins,
A barrier of bigotry bars the way in.

At the frontier of the mind,
Where my 'caste' ends, and yours begins,
A rugged reef repels relations.

At the frontier of the mind,
Where your colour ends, and mine begins,
Rigid ramparts rear their ranks.

At the frontier of the mind,
Where my faith ends, and your begins,
Fanatic flames flare.

Once upon a distant dream-time,
I flew upon a winged thought
To a mind without frontiers,
And breathed the fresh air of free ideas,
And wandered in a country without borders.

Give me more minds without frontiers,
More countries without barriers,
Where the unfettered flow of ideas
Mingles with the air of empathy.

FOR A LITTLE SYRIAN BOY

"Postern of Fate, the Desert Gate, Disaster's
Cavern, Fort of Fear."

> *The Gates Of Damascus*
> *James Elroy Flecker*

 It's an ill wind, the west wind, full of hate
cries,
From Afghanistan to Iraq,
From Palestine to Syria…
Will it stop at the sea?

I do not know your name,
Was it Ali, Aziz or Ahmed?
I only know you lived in Syria ,
And that you were three years old.

Were? At the age of three?
I only know your last words:
"I will tell God everything."
What will you tell God, little one?

That the air in your village is black with
smoke and evil?
That it rains bombs instead of hail-stones?
That your sister died after drinking the water
from the well?
Will you tell Him that you were only playing
with your baby-brother when it happened?
That you saw your father on fire, your
brother's body blown,
Heard your mother screaming, and felt your
head exploding?

Will you tell God that you said your namaz
Five times a day, as the mullahs told you to?
Will you ask God what your fault was, your
family's fault was,
For this terrible punishment?

God be thy guide from camp to camp,
God be thy shade from well to well...

And innocent one, will you ask God
To take care of your mother, as she has no-
one else?

THE MISSING GUINEA-PIG

"One flew east, and one flew west,
 And one flew over the cuckoo's nest."

Four little guinea-pigs went for a walk,
By and by they lost their way
And found themselves in a concrete jungle;
Seeing a sign-board: "Asylum",
They entered the gates
Without reading the small-print:
"Dystopia."

There was a pond,
With ducks paddling in the muddied water,
Mirroring the lame-ducks
Waddling inside.

They soon realized they were trapped,
As they were not allowed to leave.
Any question they asked was countered with:
"We have to ask the Boss."

The Boss was a looming presence whom no-
one ever got to meet.

They were mechanically screened and strait-
jacketed,
Pigeon-holed and case-historied,
Without a single human touch.

One little guinea-pig was labelled bi-polar,
Another, autistic,
A third, schizophrenic,
But the fourth defied labels.

The first guinea-pig was given shock-therapy,
The second, lobotomized,
The third, robotised.
He eventually became so used to his cell,
Like the Prisoner Of Chillon,
That he did not want to leave.

But they were at their wits' end
About what to do with the fourth one,
For he defied regimentation,
And jumped over the barricade of their
collective will.

Soon there was a new notice on the wall
outside:
"Rs. One crore reward for the missing guinea-
pig."

NEW-AGE ALGEBRA

Time was, when I enjoyed Algebra,
I loved balancing factors,
Solving equations,
Fault=blame,
Fault+blame=accountability,
Accountability + responsibility= punishment,
Fault+ punishment=justice.

In the New Age Algebra,
Fault=shifting the blame;
The fault is *yours*,
But *I* am the scape-goat.

Accountabilty is a missing factor,
In its grammar, money+ego=power,
It's partner, geometry is too jagged, too
angular.
Power + exploitation= success;
Ego+ misuse of power=heady cocktail;
But insolent Might over committed Right can
never =justice.

I have had enough of the New Age Algebra,
Give me the old values,
Give me the old equations,
Above all, give me justice.

MOTHER EARTH

Your sons have hacked your body,
And divided you into five continents,
Your daughters have been confined to sandy
shores.

One son flexes his nuclear muscles against his
own parents,
Another bars the doors of his house to his
children;
One daughter spews out her tensions through
tsunamis,
Another heaves sighs of hurricanes.

Your children are killing each other,
They have ravaged every part of your body,
And are depleting you of all your energies,
And you are sobbing your guts out through
earth-quakes;
How will you survive, Mother?

Vishva Dharini,
If you die, who will live,
If you live, who will die?
*Dharmarakshathi, rakshathah.**

*Dharma protects those who protect it.

"Wayfarer, there is no way-
Only foam-trails to the sea."
Antonio Machado

MOSAIC

A sun-bird sweeps skyward
On a sublime arc of sound;
A leaf lingers
On a rippling wave of light,
A flower flutters down,
Its soul soars into space.

A butterfly?
A bird of paradise?

The flame of the forest
Bursts into sparks,
From its glowing embers
A firebird flies free.

A tree is felled,
Its ragged roots hug the hill-side:
A human life is hushed,
A new-born baby cries.

Where does leaf end, and flower begin?

Where does butterfly end, and bird begin?
Where does root end, and tree begin,
And where does death end, and life begin?

NIRVANA

Coincidence or inter-connection,
 Synchronicity or cosmic design,
Your compass is too colossal to be confined
        to the cage of words.

 If this is a glimpse of the nirvana that sages
        speak of,
Sweep me where you will
In your mystic flow.
I surrender-
I, a whisper in the wind,
Wait, trembling, tremulous, for the embrace
        of the whirl-wind.

MRG TRISHNA

"Kasturi kudal base
Mrg dhonde ban mahi."
                              Kabir
(Kasturi musk is located within the deer's own self,
Bur the deer searches all over the forest for it.)

Last night I had a strange dream-
I dreamt of a musk deer, a *Kasturi mrg,*
Which was searching frantically for the
                fragrance
That was driving her to frenzy.

She sniffed the breeze,
She searched the ground,
She scoured the skies,
She hit her horns against the trees,
But could not find the source
Of the maddening musk.

When her fellow-deer went grazing,

She did not join them, for her hunger was for
        something else;
When they went to the stream to quench their
        thirst,
She stayed behind,
For her *trishna* was of another nature.
Slowly she began to pine and waste away.

One day, a wise old deer passed by,
He perceived the plight of the poor musk
        deer,
And shook his head.
"Stop searching , he advised,
For what you seek is a mystic mirage,
The day you find it, you will die."

The poor musk deer became even more
        obsessed
With the source of the elusive scent;
She kept yearning, and languishing,
Then, in a gleam of insight,
She saw a blue haze, shimmering with an
        ethereal light;
Magnetised by its magic power,
She walked towards it;
And saw a musk deer,
A fellow Kasturi Mrg
Reflected in its depths.

"Sister of my soul", she said

"Can you please tell me from where
This maddening scent is coming from?
I have searched everywhere,
But have not been able to find it.

There was silence for a long minute,
Then the other spoke:
"Oh foolish one,
You have searched everywhere,
But in the right place.
I too have been consumed by *mrg thrishna* for
        long,
And have searched and searched;
I finally found it in my #*hrdaya pundarika*".

"Sister of my heart,"
Said the musk deer,
Please help me find this secret place,"
As she joined the other.

When I awoke from my dream,
I saw in a fractal flash
That the image in the mirage was myself.

*The yearning of the musk-deer
#space within the heart.